the best of Stereophonics

GW00370897

the bartender and the thief 2

hurry up and wait 7

i stopped to fill my car up 12

i wouldn't believe your radio 22

just looking 15

local boy in the photograph 28

more life in a tramp's vest 52

pick a part that's new 34

a thousand trees 40

traffic 46

exclusive distributors:
music sales limited, 8/9 frith street, london w1v 5tz, england.
music sales pty limited, 120 rothschild avenue, rosebery, nsw 2018, australia.
order no.am963919
isbn 0-7119-8150-7
this book © copyright 2000 by wise publications.

music arranged by derek jones.
music engraved by paul ewers music design.
compiled by nick crispin.
photographs courtesy of rex features and all action.

printed in great britain by printwise (haverhill) limited, suffolk

your guarantee of quality:
as publishers, we strive to produce every book to the highest commercial standards.
the music has been freshly engraved and the book has been carefully designed to
minimise awkward page turns and to make playing from it a real pleasure.
particular care has been given to specifying acid-free,
neutral-sized paper made from pulps which have not been elemental chlorine bleached.
this pulp is from farmed sustainable forests and was produced with special regard for the environment.
throughout, the printing and binding have been planned to ensure a sturdy,
attractive publication which should give years of enjoyment.
if your copy fails to meet our high standards, please inform us and we will gladly replace it.

music sales' complete catalogue describes thousands of titles and
is available in full colour sections by subject, direct from music sales limited.
please state your areas of interest and send a cheque/postal order for £1.50 for postage to:
music sales limited, newmarket road, bury st. edmunds, suffolk ip33 3yb.

www.musicsales.com

wise publications
london/new york/sydney/paris/copenhagen/madrid/tokyo

the bartender and the thief

words by kelly jones
music by kelly jones, richard jones & stuart cable

-dies dis-mem-bered. Saved what they stole to meet___ at the al-tar,

place where they first set eyes___ on each oth-er. Flew to the sun to start___

___ life all ov-er, set up a bar and robbed___ all the lo-cals.

5

Verse 2:
He watched the lesbian talk
She kissed and groped but mostly talked in lust
Crushed
He couldn't make the call
His eyes were gripped on licking tongues, enough's enough
Failed for once
Long diggin', gone fishin', love drinkin'.

The bartender and the thief *etc.*

hurry up and wait

words by kelly jones
music by kelly jones, richard jones & stuart cable

1. Wait to wake, to get a ride in the rain, buy a tick-et they can check, we can claim, so we don't spend what's our own.

For a seat, a place to stop, a green light, a red

cross, run a-round nak-ed do-ing old things like the ones be - fore.____

2. For a break so you can take a lit-tle some-thing that-'ll make your next break come a lit-tle quick-er than the
(Verses 3 & 4 see block lyrics)

ones be - fore._____

For an an - swer spy a sweet dan - cer, she walks from the door of the hall, wish you wait-ed for your

wed - ding_____ vows._____

So hur - ry up_____ and wait,_____ but what's worth wait - ing for?__

So hur - ry up_____ and wait,__

_____ but what's worth wait - ing for?_____

1, 2.

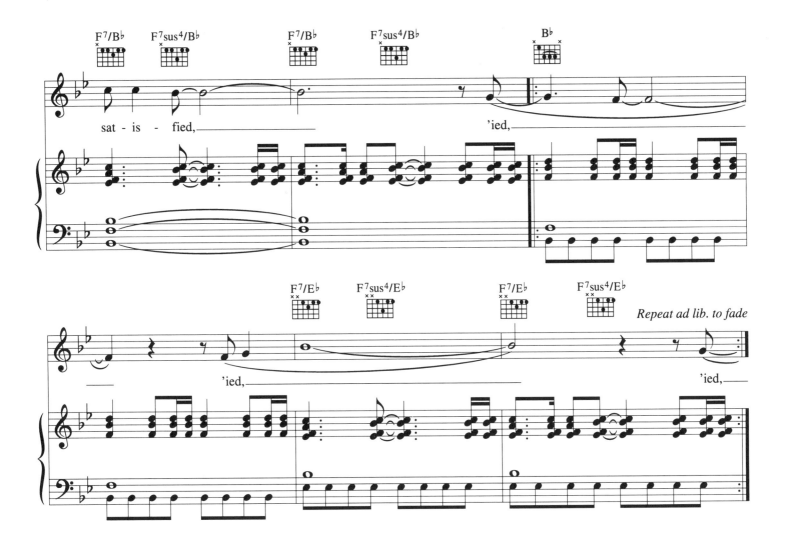

Verse 3:
We wait to get warm, the car starts from cold stall
To make a first move magazines made the rules to make us lose
For your dream man, the house you could both plan, the car in the sales
Add the wet dream with the man you wish that you had.

So hurry up and wait etc.

Verse 4:
A watched pot never boils, sugar seconds to dissolve
Feel your appetite loss, food's relevance lost inside
We wait to get there, and when we get there
We wait around for anyone to tell us what we even got there for.

So hurry up and wait *etc.*

i stopped to fill my car up

words by kelly jones
music by kelly jones, richard jones & stuart cable

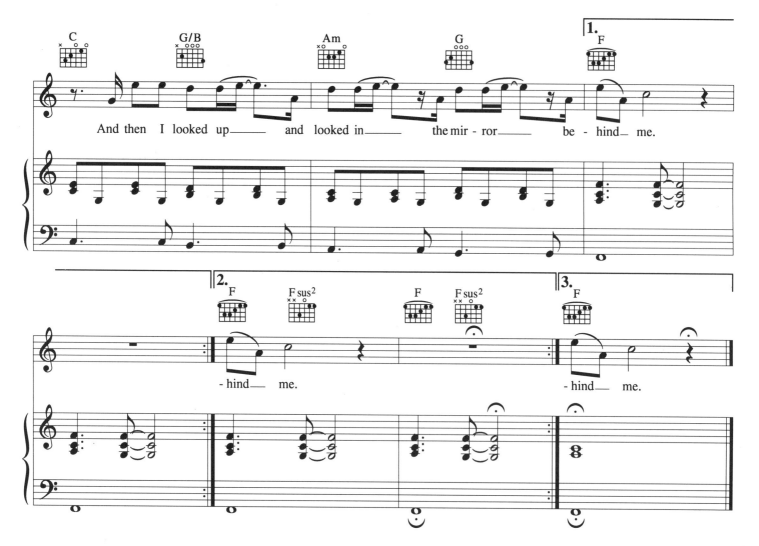

And then I looked up＿ and looked in＿ the mir - ror＿ be - hind＿ me.

- hind＿ me.

- hind＿ me.

Verse 2:

A man 'round forty in the back seat
Must have stepped in when I was empty
So why's he sat there just waiting?
Likely to smash my face in!
He had a bag full of money
He said "Just drive me away"
I didn't know where I was going
Yet it felt good to be strange
And still I look up and look in
The mirror behind me
And still I look up and look in
The mirror behind me.

Verse 3:

Curiosity is over
He stepped down from the car
He pulled a gun from his jacket
Said I was going to die
It gives me so much satisfaction
To watch you beg and cry
Well, I just made up this story
To get your attention
Makes me smile!
I never looked up or looked in
The mirror behind me
I never looked up or looked in
The mirror behind me.

just looking

words by kelly jones
music by kelly jones, richard jones & stuart cable

1. There's things I ___ want, ___ there's things I ___ think ___ I want. There's things I've ___

I'm not buy - ing.____ I'm just

look - ing,____ keeps me smil - ing____

Verse 3:
A house I seen
Another coulda' been
You drenched my head
And said what I said
You said that life is what you make of it
Yet most of us just fake.

And I'm just looking *etc.*

%:
There's things I want
There's things I think I want
There's things I've had
There's things I wanna have
They say the more you fly
The more you risk your life.

Well I'm looking *etc.*

i wouldn't believe your radio

words by kelly jones
music by kelly jones, richard jones & stuart cable

tun - nel un - der - sea,_____ you nev - er know, if it

cracks in half,_____ you're nev - er ev - er gon - na see me._____

But you can have it all if you like._____

You can have it all if you like,_____ and you can pay for it the rest of your_

Verse 2:
I wouldn't believe your wireless radio
If I had myself a flying giraffe
You'd have one in a box with a window.

But you can have it all *etc.*

local boy in the photograph

words by kelly jones
music by kelly jones, richard jones & stuart cable

1. There's no mis - take,— I smell that smell,— it's that time— of year— a - gain;
(Verses 2 & 3 see block lyrics)

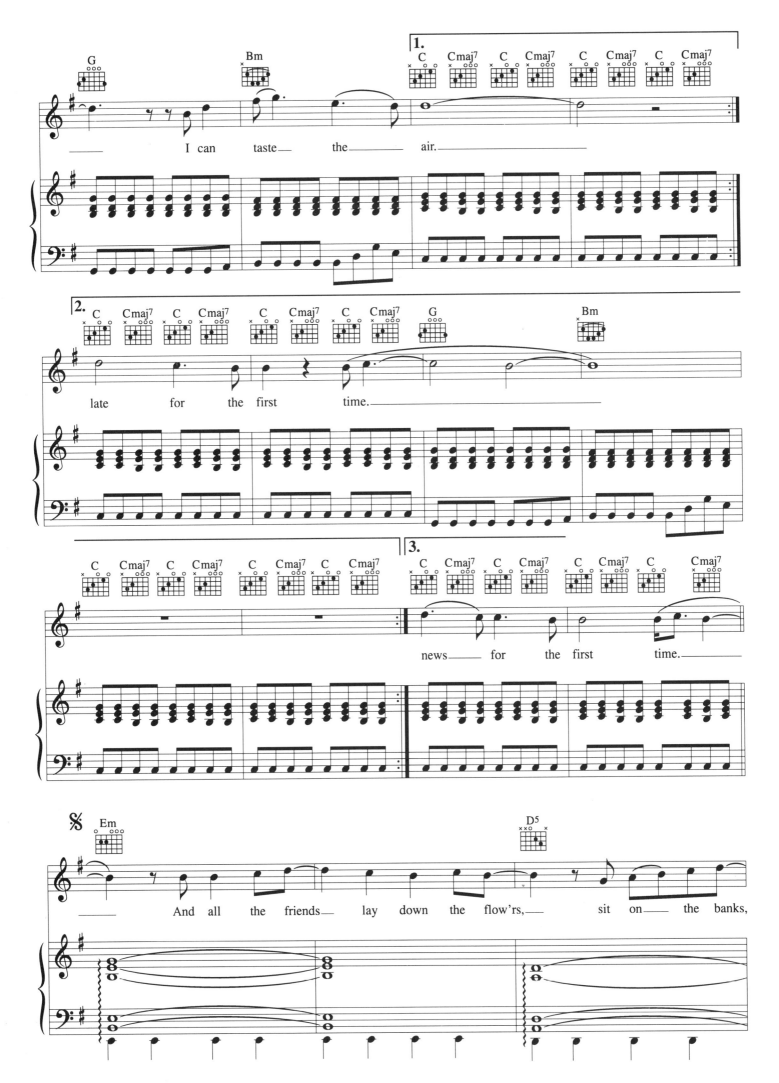

29

5. There's no mis-take___ I smell that smell,___ it's that time
(Verse 6 see block lyric)

___ of year___ a - gain;___ I can taste___ the air.___

1.

2.

late___ for the

D.%. al Coda

first time to - day.___

32

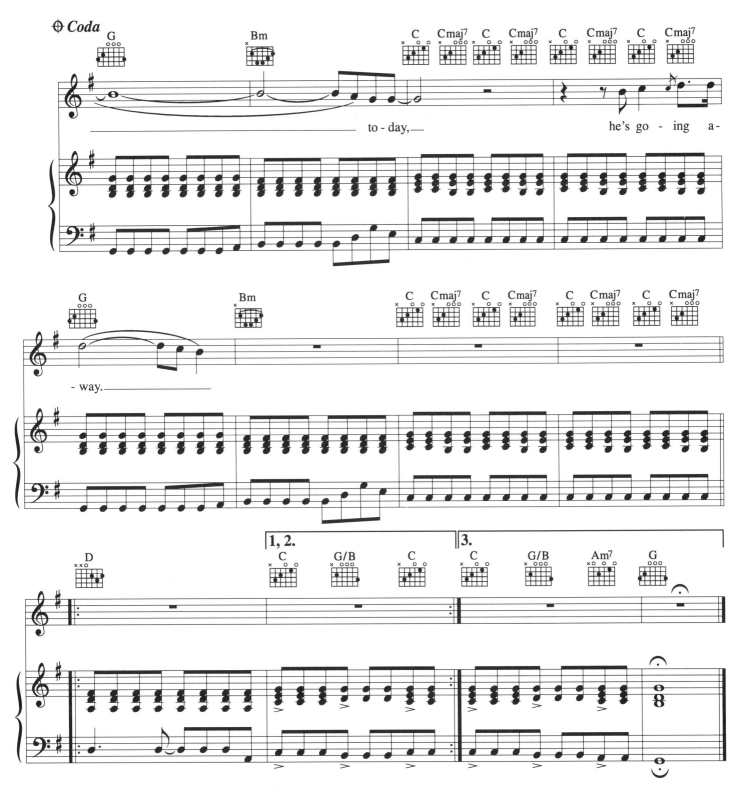

Verse 2:
The clocks go back, railway track
Something blocks the line again
And the train runs late for the first time.

Verse 3:
A pebble beach, we're underneath
Pier just been painted red
Where I heard the news for the first time.

Verse 6:
The clocks go back, railway track
Something blocks the line again
And the train runs late for the first time today.

pick a part that's new

words by kelly jones
music by kelly jones, richard jones & stuart cable

1. I've nev-er been here be-fore, I did-n't know where to go,
(Verse 2 see block lyric)

new.

So what's new to you?

What's new to you?

What's new to you?

Verse 2:
People drinking on their own
Push buttons on the phone
Was I here once before
Is that my voice on the phone
Last drink on my own
Did I ever leave at all
Confusions familiar.

You can do all things *etc.*

a thousand trees

words by kelly jones
music by kelly jones, richard jones & stuart cable

school-yard, in the scrap-yard, in the chip shop, in the phone box, in the

pool hall, at the shoe stall, ev-'ry cor-ner turn'd a-round.— 2. Start-ed with a

school-girl who was run-ning, run-ning home to her mam and dad;— told them she was
(Verses 3 & 4 see block lyrics)

play-ing in the change-room of her lo-cal foot-ball side. They said "Tell us a-gain."

growing seeds; don't be - lieve why he's

been a - way.

D.%. al Coda

4. In the

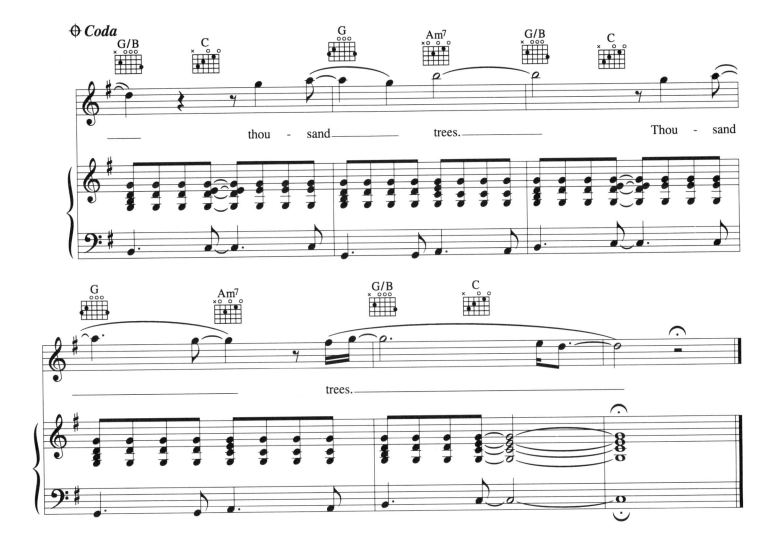

⊕ *Coda*

thou - sand trees. Thou - sand

trees.

Verse 3:
See it in the classroom, or the swimming pool
Where the matchstick men are made
At the Scout's hall, at the football
Where the wise we trust are paid
They all honour his name
"Did a lot for the game"
He had his name knocked up above the sports ground gates
Now they're ripping them down
Stamping the ground
Picture gathers dust in the bar in the lounge.

It takes one tree *etc.*

Verse 4:
In the school yard, change room
Playing fields, bathroom
Phone box, office blocks
Corners turned around
They keep doubting the flame
Tossing the blame
Got his name knocked up above the sports ground gates
Now they're ripping them down
Stamping the ground
Picture gathers dust in the bar in the lounge.

It takes one tree *etc.*

traffic

words by kelly jones
music by kelly jones, richard jones & stuart cable

1. We all face the same—

—— way,—— still it takes all—— day;— I take a look to my——
(Verses 2 & 3 see block lyrics)

Wait ta - bles for a crook who wrote a hard - back____ book. D'you teach kids how to____ read, or sell your bo - dy on their__ street? A nurse with - out____ a job?__ An - oth - er up - town__ snob? But have I got you all____

Verse 2:
Another office affair, to kill an unborn scare
You talk dirty to a priest, it makes them human at least
But is she running away to start a brand new day?
Or's she going home? Why's she driving alone?

Is anyone going anywhere *etc.*

Verse 3:
She got a body in the boot, or just bags full of food?
Those are model's legs; but are they women's, are they men's?
She shouts down the phone, missed a payment on the loan
She gotta be above the rest, keeping up with the best.

Is anyone going anythere *etc.*

more life in a tramp's vest

words by kelly jones
music by kelly jones, richard jones & stuart cable

2. They al-ways moan,   moan it's not so cheap;   cheap-er still,
(Verse 3 see block lyirc)

cheap-er still down the street.— Lost my rag and tell them "Take your bag and shop down there."

——— Clos-ing down,   they're clos-ing down a-no-ther road;— one-way

sys-tem— steals the show. Mac the Knife swigs a can and sings the day a-way. There's

tramp's vest.—   There's more life,   more life,

To Coda ⊕ D   E

more   life— a   in a   tramp's   vest.—

A   Dmaj⁷

Bm⁷   Dsus²   Bm⁷

I get camp - ing eyes in the fi - al hour. Last min - ute

shop-pers pick-ing cau - li-flow'r. Mac the Knife swigs a can and sings the day a - way. There's

tramp's vest.___

Verse 2:
The flower man sits down in the street
Surrounded by stock he bought back last week
Bring back the ladies wearing lipstick on their teeth
Make up, we make up a crappy joke
Sit back, relax and have a smoke
Mac the Knife swigs a can and sings the day away.

There's more life *etc.*